HORRIBLE SCIENCE

ANNUAL 2008

THIS BOOK
BELONGS TO:

SCHOLASTIC

DEAR READER...

Your beastly body is an amazing invention – and it's home to a whole host of sensational and sickening surprises. From your bulging brain to your disgusting digestive system, bloody body bits and startling senses, it's full of foul features and fantastic functions. Read on to discover the torrid truth about the horrid human body – but beware, it's not for the faint-hearted...

CONTENTS

BEWARE OF DANGER!

SPLURB!

BEWARE OF MESSY EXPERIMENT

BULGING BRAINS

Your bulging brain is divided into departments that each have their own job. Step inside the IQ HQ...

The cerebrum (ser—ee—brum) and its outer layer, the **cortex** is the largest section of the brain and is used for its most complicated jobs. The front part deals with problem solving (**1**), planning (**2**) and self-control (**3**). The noisy speech centre (**4**) is tucked in behind. A strip of brain matter across the middle of the cortex (**5a**) controls movement. Just behind this 'motor shop' are the touch sensors (**5b**).

Hearing takes place lower in the cortex (**6**) and sight at the rear (**7**). Information gathered in these parts is passed to the 'associations centre' (**8**) where the brain makes connections between what you see and hear and stuff stored in your memory. These connections are passed to the understanding department (**9**).

The limbic system is buried deep in the brain, surrounded by the cerebrum. It deals with emotions and complicated brain functions. The smell centre (**10**) is like a tiny bulb. The hypothalamus (hi—po—thal—a—mus) (**11**) is the head office's control centre. The pituitary (pit—you—it—ary) gland (**12**) follows orders from the control centre.

The 'fight or flight' instinct is kept in the amygdala (am—ig—dala) (**13**). The hippocampus (**14**) helps the brain to organise and store memories. The pineal (pin—knee—al) gland (**15**) tells the body when to wake up and when to go to sleep.

The cerebellum (ser—ee—bell—um) (**16**) coordinates body movement and balance while the body's automatic functions (like breathing) are run by the brainstem (**17**).

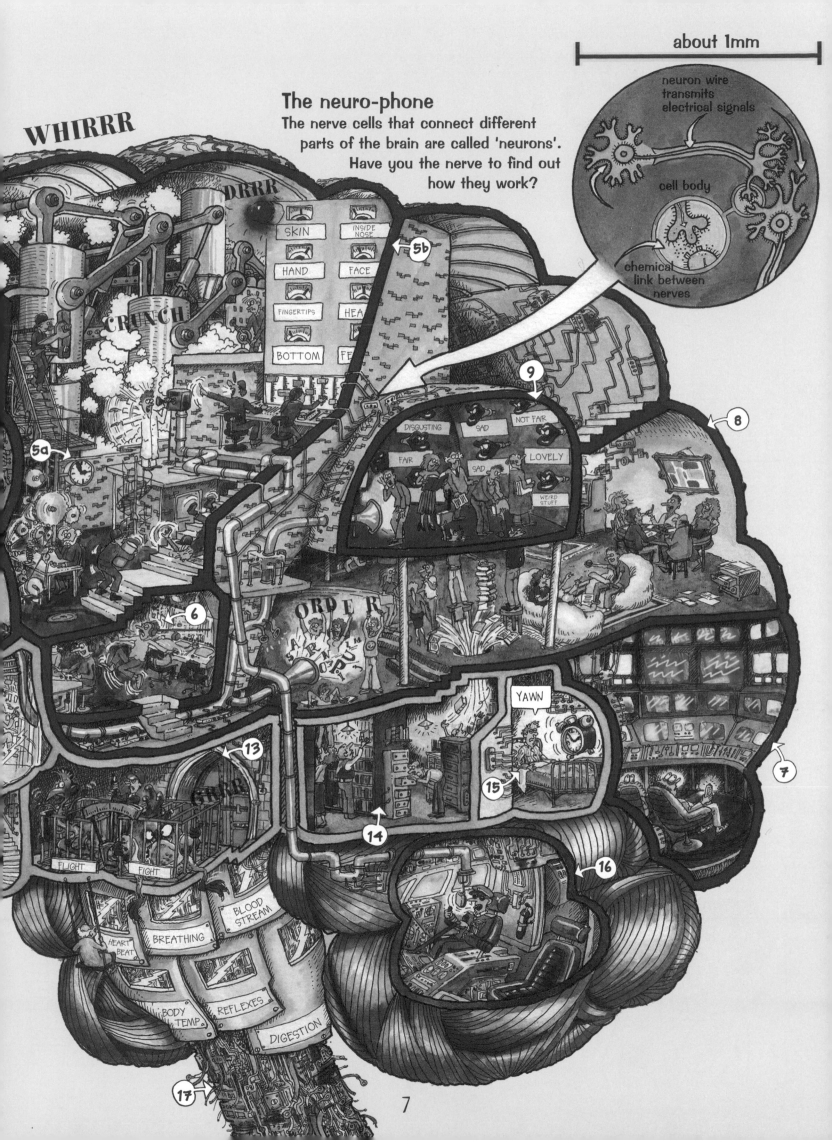

THE STRANGE STORY OF EINSTEIN'S BRAIN

Albert Einstein had one of the twentieth century's most brilliant brains but, when he died in 1955, he lost his mind… quite literally!

APRIL 17TH 1955. PRINCETON HOSPITAL, USA.

IT'S THE CUTTING EDGE OF SCIENCE!

BZZZZZ!

DR THOMAS HARVEY WAS THE PATHOLOGIST ENTRUSTED WITH CONDUCTING THE AUTOPSY ON THE BODY OF THE LATE GREAT SCIENTIST, ALBERT EINSTEIN.

HARVEY WAS DETERMINED TO DISCOVER THE SECRET OF EINSTEIN'S INCREDIBLE INTELLECT. ONCE HE'D SAWN OPEN HIS SKULL, HE CAREFULLY SCOOPED OUT THE CRINKLY CONTENTS…

SCHLURP!

YUCK! HE WAS CERTAINLY BRAINY!

…AND, DESPITE EINSTEIN'S STRICT INSTRUCTIONS TO DISPOSE OF HIS BRAIN ALONG WITH THE REST OF HIS BODY, HARVEY DECIDED TO HAVE IT FOR HIMSELF.

I FEEL A BIT LIGHT-HEADED

WHILE THE REST OF THE BRAINY BOFFIN'S BODY WAS REDUCED TO ASHES, HARVEY GOT HIS BULGING BRAIN SLICED INTO MORE THAN 200 PIECES AND PRESERVED THEM IN FORMALDEHYDE.

WITHIN A YEAR OF GETTING HIS HANDS ON ALBERT EINSTEIN'S MAGNIFICENT MIND, DR HARVEY HAD LOST HIS JOB, AND HIS WIFE.

I MARRIED YOU NOT FOR YOUR LOOKS, BUT FOR YOUR BRAINS. WHAT A MISTAKE!

I'M IN A BIT OF A PICKLE!

BUT EINSTEIN'S BRAIN BROUGHT DR HARVEY NOTHING BUT BAD LUCK…

BUT WHAT HAPPENED TO THE ECCENTRIC EGGHEAD'S BRAIN AFTER THAT REMAINED A MYSTERY FOR MORE THAN TWENTY YEARS…

BULGING BRAIN BASICS

The brain is the part of your body that tells you what's going on around you. You can use your brain to order your body around and even to order everybody else around. But there's much more to your brain. Much, much more.

The brain is always busy. Even when it doesn't seem to be doing much your brain is crackling with the electrical force of millions of nerves. It fires off signals, feelings, orders and thoughts at incredible speed. And that's not all…

Inside your brain are your precious memories, your dreams, your hopes for the future and the knowledge of everything you love and care about. In your brain you can sense lovely smells and tastes and colours. Your brain helps you feel great and happy about life and that's the good side. But your brain also creates horrible fears and worries that can make you miserable.

IT MAKES YOU THINK, DOESN'T IT?

Your brain makes the thoughts and feelings that make your personality. Your brain turns your body from a living object into you the person. Without it you'd be as dead as a dodo's tombstone, so it's good to know that you've got your very own bulging brain right now between your ears… hopefully.

Now you've found out a bit about what the bulging brain does, you're ready to check out how it works…

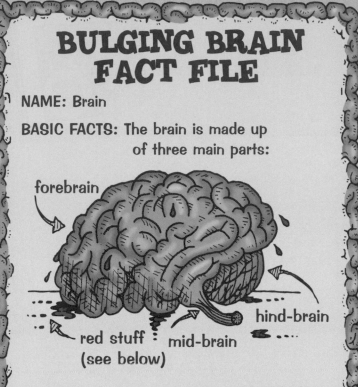

BULGING BRAIN FACT FILE

NAME: Brain

BASIC FACTS: The brain is made up of three main parts:

forebrain

red stuff (see below)

mid-brain

hind-brain

Each area is made up of smaller bits with different jobs.

DISGUSTING DETAILS: The brain needs energy from the sugar and oxygen carried in the blood. So it sucks in about 750ml of the red stuff every minute. All this hot blood gives out lots of heat – that's why your brain is the hottest part of your body.  It weighs about 1.3kg – that's about the weight of a large bag of sugar. In fact, the brain is only one-fiftieth the weight of a grown-up man and it's far lighter than your guts, your blood, your skin or your bones.

Dare you discover... why the brain is wrinkly?

Ever wondered why brains are wrinkly? Now's your chance to discover the answer...

All you do is:

1. Screw one sheet of paper into a tight ball.

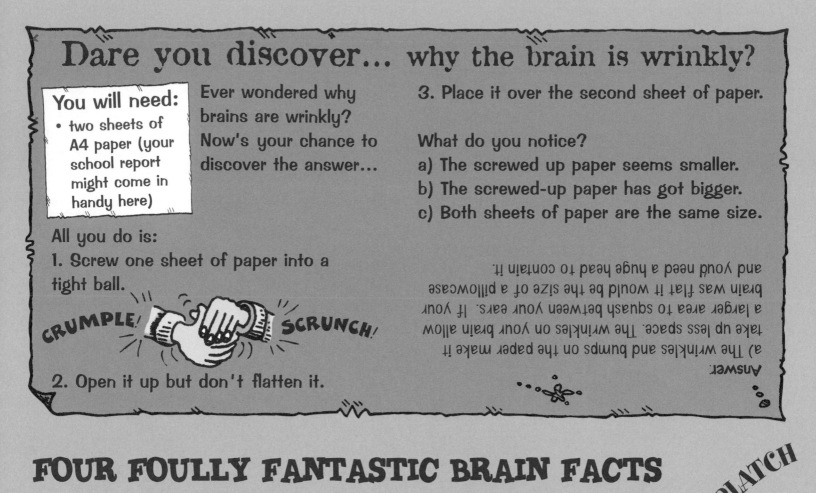

CRUMPLE! SCRUNCH!

2. Open it up but don't flatten it.

3. Place it over the second sheet of paper.

What do you notice?

a) The screwed up paper seems smaller.
b) The screwed-up paper has got bigger.
c) Both sheets of paper are the same size.

Answer:
a) The wrinkles and bumps on the paper make it take up less space. The wrinkles on your brain allow a larger area to squash between your ears. If your brain was flat it would be the size of a pillowcase and you'd need a huge head to contain it.

FOUR FOULLY FANTASTIC BRAIN FACTS

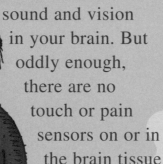

SQUIDGE

1 Your nerves take signals from elsewhere in your body to your brain. This means you experience pain, touch, taste, smell, sound and vision in your brain. But oddly enough, there are no touch or pain sensors on or in the brain tissue itself. So, it's nice to know that if someone stuck his or her finger in your brain and waggled it about, you wouldn't feel a thing – honest!

2 In the 1960s an operation which cut the brain in two was performed on some patients who suffered violent fits. The operation stopped the fits, but afterwards the two sides of the brain acted like separated people. One woman tried to put on a different shirt with each hand. She ended up wearing two shirts.

SPLATCH

3 Your brain feels like squidgy blancmange or a soft-boiled egg.
The brain needs water for vital chemical reactions like sending nerve signals. Without water, it begins to overheat and starts to see things that aren't there. Ultimately it'll die.

4 Scientist Louis Sokoloff of the US National Institute of Mental Health has found that the brain uses the same amount of energy gazing dreamily at a sunset as it does in a tough science test. And how much energy is that? Well it's just about enough to power a light bulb.

IT'S YEAR 5... WE WON'T NEED OUR SUNGLASSES

IT'S A KNOCKOUT!

Your brain's about as hard as jelly so imagine if it didn't have any protection. Eventually, every bang, prod and nod would turn your grey matter into gooey mush. Luckily, your head's got some built-in safety features to stop you losing your mind!

1

2

3

GRRRN!

URGH!

BOING!

CLONK!

BULGING BRAIN FACT FILE

NAME: Consciousness

BASIC FACTS: It means being aware of your thoughts and feelings. Scientists aren't sure how this happens. The whole of your cortex (the outer layer of your brain) seems to be involved in making you aware of your thoughts and what they mean.

DISGUSTING DETAILS: People can lose consciousness after a bad accident and stay in this state – it's called a coma – for years.

NAME: Sleep

BASIC FACTS: When you go to sleep you lose consciousness and you're unaware of your surroundings.

DISGUSTING DETAILS: Staying awake for two weeks can kill you. Without rest, the body gets more exhausted and vital functions like heartbeat begin to falter.

GROAN

MOAN

WHAT'S ON YOUR MIND?

1. Getting up suddenly in the morning gives your brain a nasty shock, as it throws your brain forward inside your skull.

2. But don't panic – your skull bones act like a set of shock-absorbers to stop your brain getting bashed about.

3. Under the skull there's also a protective layer called the meninges (muh–nin–jeez). It's actually made of three layers of thick tissue separated by fluid – this soaks up the shock of any bumps and protects the brain. Your brain 'floats' in this fluid.

4. The effects of an injury can depend on which part of the brain gets damaged. It can lead to problems reading, smelling or tasting, or amnesia – that's loss of memory, remember?

5. Headaches are brain-pains. When you're under stress, more blood squirts into your brain, stretching the sides of the blood vessels (5a). The expanded vessels, which are carrying more blood cells (5b), cause your head to ache.

RIGHT VS LEFT?

You've heard of people being left-handed or right-footed, but how can you be left-eyed right-eyed? It depends on which side of your brain is stronger. Here's how to find out which one you are...

You will need:
- a finger (preferably one of your own)
- two eyes (these should definitely be your own)
- a pen

1 The first step is easy – even a parent could do it! Hold a pen out at arm's length.

2 Using your other hand, stick your finger a short distance from your nose – but don't be tempted to pick it!

3 Position the finger so that it's in line with the pen – the finger should look out of focus. You should be able to see the pen through the finger.

4 Now wink each of your eyes in turn. It's best not to do this in public, people might think you're winking at them!

5 What should you see? When you wink one eye, the finger stays where it is and blocks the pen completely.

6 And when you wink the other eye, the finger jumps sideways. What does this mean? When the finger didn't move and blocked the pen, you were using your dominant eye — this is the one that does most of the seeing when both eyes are used together. So if you're looking through your right eye when this happens (with your left eye shut), you're right-eyed, and if you're using your left eye... you've guessed it... you're left-eyed!

Become a mind reader!

1 Once you've found someone willing to have their mind read, here's what you tell them to do...

THINK OF A NUMBER BETWEEN 1 AND 10. OK, NOW MULTIPLY IT BY 9. IF YOU'VE GOT A TWO-DIGIT NUMBER*, ADD THE TWO NUMBERS TOGETHER. NOW SUBTRACT 5.

*e.g. if you've got 27, add 2 + 7, which = 9

2 Then say to them...

IF ALL THE LETTERS IN THE ALPHABET WERE NUMBERED, 'A' WOULD BE NUMBER 1, 'B' NUMBER 2 AND SO ON. THINK OF WHAT LETTER OF THE ALPHABET YOUR NUMBER IS BUT DON'T TELL ME. NOW THINK OF A COUNTRY THAT STARTS WITH THAT LETTER

3 Remember, don't rush them...

TAKE THE SECOND LETTER IN THAT COUNTRY'S NAME AND THINK OF AN ANIMAL WHOSE NAME BEGINS WITH IT. USE THE FIRST ANIMAL THAT COMES INTO YOUR HEAD. NOW, WHAT COLOUR ARE THOSE ANIMALS?

4 Pause here while you look like you are concentrating. Then say...

THAT'S FUNNY... THIS CAN'T BE RIGHT... THERE AREN'T ANY GREY ELEPHANTS IN DENMARK!

WARNING!
The only chance it won't work is if they mess up the arithmetic or think of some bizarre country beginning with 'D' – so don't try it on a geography teacher!

Go to the Puzzle answers on page 60 to see how this trick works.

BUMPS 'N' BASHES

Everything about your brain is baffling, bemusing and bewildering. But these tales of bumps, bangs and bashes may leave you brain-bogglingly bamboozled...

Foul Footie Facts

- It's possible to run around and perform simple actions while unconscious. In the 1956 FA Cup Final goalkeeper Bert Trautmann was knocked unconscious in a collision with an opposing player. But battling Bert somehow made a save and completed the game.

- In 1997, Vicky, a 10-year-old British girl, banged her head and started writing backwards and upside-down. Vicky could read her own writing but it must have baffled her teacher. A year later she banged her head while watching football. The next day, her writing had returned to normal.

- In 1998, a retired Scottish footballer said that his memory loss was due to heading the ball too much. His wife said that he often forgot who he was talking to. Before the 1950s, footballs were made of heavy leather and when it rained they sucked in water and got heavier. If they hit you on the head they could knock you out.

What a Pain!

If you lived in the Stone Age you might be tempted to keep quiet about any problems involving your head. Brain surgery Stone Age-style was likely to leave you rather more sore than before.

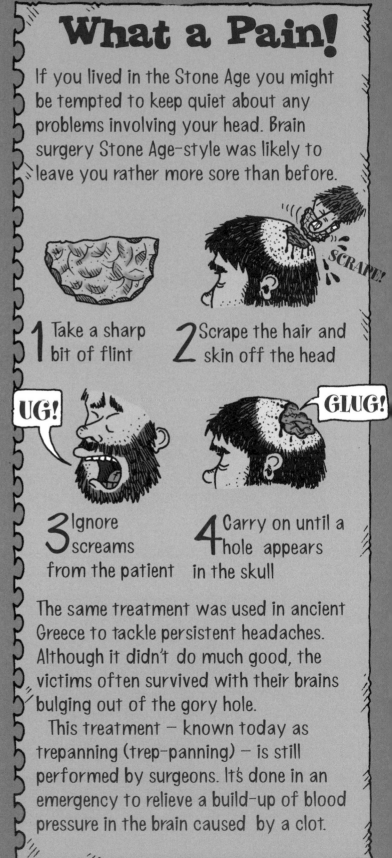

1 Take a sharp bit of flint

2 Scrape the hair and skin off the head

3 Ignore screams from the patient

4 Carry on until a hole appears in the skull

The same treatment was used in ancient Greece to tackle persistent headaches. Although it didn't do much good, the victims often survived with their brains bulging out of the gory hole.

This treatment – known today as trepanning (trep-panning) – is still performed by surgeons. It's done in an emergency to relieve a build-up of blood pressure in the brain caused by a clot.

BEASTLY BRAINTEASERS

These baffling brainbenders will give your mind-muscles a good stretch.

Mirror Muddle

Here's a monster maze with an extra twist. You'll need a hand-held mirror and a pencil. Hold the mirror so that you can see a reflection of the maze in it. Then, looking only at the reflection, draw a route to the centre! Sounds easy? Just you try it!

READ THIS IN THE MIRROR

CAN YOU HELP THE MONSTER BACK TO BARON FRANKENSTEIN'S CASTLE AVOIDING THE OTHER MONSTERS ON THE WAY?

EEK!

SCREAM!

HOWL!

SLOBBER!

DRIBBLE!

ROAR!

HISS!

GROWL!

COME HOME MONSTER!

SPOT THE DIFFERENCE
Can you spot the six differences in the pictures below?

OUCH!

OUCH!

Turn to page 60 to see the answers.

17

STARTLING SENSES

The Horrible Science Stimulator is giving these kids an ultra-realistic scary cinema experience!

SIGHT

1. The kids are watching a scene where it looks like they're falling down a crocodile pit on the end of a bungee cord. The screen has a 3-dimensional effect, which makes the crocs even scarier!

TOUCH

2. To create the feeling of falling and bouncing up again, the chairs have been fitted with hydraulic lifts that rise and fall fast. Hold tight!

3. Hands and feet are attached to special sensors connected to a revolving disk containing objects that enhance the feel of the scene. These are false teeth like the croc gnashers (**3a**), sandpaper like rough croc skin (**3b**), warm milk like blood (**3c**), and pasta and sausages to feel like guts (**3d**).

SMELL

4. To get those nostrils twitching, special air vents pipe in odours that recreate the reeking croc pit! The smells include a sweaty wrestler with hairy armpits (**4a**) to heighten heat and fear: rotting meat (**4b**) to smell like the flesh of chomped humans; a big pile of poo (**4c**) and a urinal (**4d**) smelling of pee are not too pleasant, and old socks (**4e**) are stinky. Some honey (**4f**) is added to keep the kids sweet!

TASTE

5. The kids are eating some cleverly-designed confectionery that alters its taste by receiving a signal from a transmitter (**5a**). In a previous scene on a snowy mountain, they tasted like ice cream. Now the smell of the croc pit is enhanced by the awful taste of dog biscuits (**5b**)!

HEARING

6. Speakers in surround sound emit noises including an axe chopping a cabbage (**6a**) to sound like a head being ripped off, some nuts being ground in a blender (**6b**) like crushed bones, a bucket of water being thrown (**6c**) like a splashing river, a cracking whip (**6d**) sounds like a thrashing croc's tail, a woman screaming (**6e**), scissors snipping like teeth (**6f**) and a pounding heartbeat (**6g**).

A SENSE-ATIONAL CRIME CAPER

The corner store's been raided and the robber's made a run for it with all the ice cream. It'll take more than a few fingerprints to catch this crooked character...

WHAT A NERVE!

Your super-sensitive skin is packed with about half a million sensors to keep you in touch with the outside world. The bad news is, they also cause you horrible aches and pains. Boo! Hiss!

Without senses life would be like sitting in a dark cupboard. But thanks to your brain you are bombarded with startling feelings, sights, sounds, smells and tastes. We'll discover more about these later, but to understand how all the senses are linked and coordinated, let's take a look at the quick-acting nerves that connect all the sensors to the brain…

NERVOUS & TWITCHY FACT FILE

NAME: Nerves

BASIC FACTS: 1. A network of nerves spreads from your brain and your spinal cord to reach every bit of your body. Their job is to carry signals from your senses to your brain and orders from your brain to get those lazy muscles moving.

2. In all you have 150,000km of nerves – enough to stretch round the Earth nearly four times. They can carry signals up to 120 metres per second.

3. An average-sized nerve is made up of thousands of nerve fibres (called 'axons').

DISGUSTING DETAILS: 1. Your nerves are always ready for action. In fact, when they send a signal they actually stop working! So it's more relaxing for your nerves when you do something than when you laze around doing nothing!

2. You can wire a battery to nerves in a chopped-off finger and make it twitch. There's one for the school science lab!

Reckless reflexes

Most signals from your nerves go to your brain to tell it what's going on in the different parts of your body. But some messages move so fast that they make you do things before you realise it and control it. These are called reflex actions. They include things that you can't stop once they start, like sneezing, coughing and dribbling. (Farting or burping are not reflexes so you've got no excuse for doing them at mealtimes!)

reflex action   reflex action   reflex action   disgusting habit

ATCHOO!   COUGH!   DRIBBLE!   BURP!

Time-saving reflexes mean you can whip your hand away from something dangerously hot, much faster than if your brain was consulted.

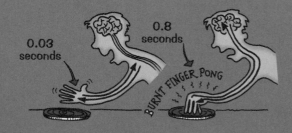

0.03 seconds   0.8 seconds   BURNT FINGER PONG

Pain is the worst thing you can sense. But you probably know all about pain already…

science homework   falling off your bike   bee stings   science tests

HOW TO USE NEURO-PHONE

The nerve system is like an amazing phone network that takes messages all around your body. Each neuron is custom built to send speedy and reliable messages ten times faster than a champion sprinter! Using your high-tech neuro-phone you can move your body, waggle your ears or slurp a milk-shake! Just do what you feel like!

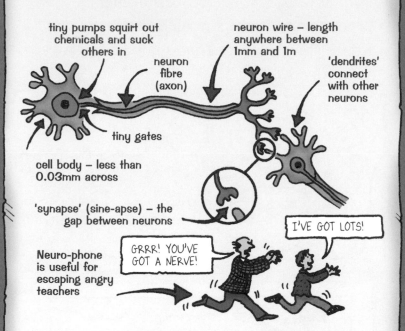

tiny pumps squirt out chemicals and suck others in

neuron fibre (axon)

neuron wire – length anywhere between 1mm and 1m

'dendrites' connect with other neurons

tiny gates

cell body – less than 0.03mm across

'synapse' (sine-apse) – the gap between neurons

Neuro-phone is useful for escaping angry teachers

GRRR! YOU'VE GOT A NERVE!

I'VE GOT LOTS!

To activate your Neuro-phone simply ask your brain cortex to send a message anywhere you want in the body. Neuro-phone will do the rest for you... here's how.

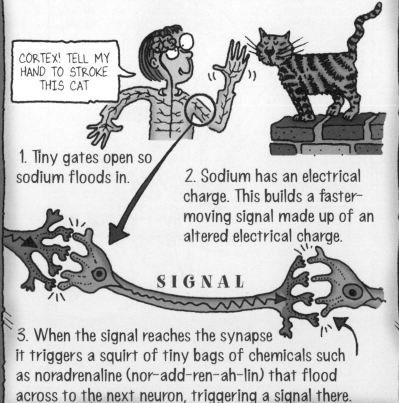

CORTEX! TELL MY HAND TO STROKE THIS CAT

1. Tiny gates open so sodium floods in.

2. Sodium has an electrical charge. This builds a faster-moving signal made up of an altered electrical charge.

SIGNAL

3. When the signal reaches the synapse it triggers a squirt of tiny bags of chemicals such as noradrenaline (nor-add-ren-ah-lin) that flood across to the next neuron, triggering a signal there.

A few painful facts

1 Pain is a big trick played by your brain on the rest of your body. Imagine you stub your toe on a stone or even the cat.

OW!

ME-OW!

You might think you feel the pain in your toe. But you actually experience it in your brain because that's where the nerve signal goes.

2 Your body is crowded with thousands of pain receptors. Obviously any damage to the body is red-hot urgent news for the brain – there may be more damage just about to occur so the pain receptors need to let the brain know what's going on NOW.

3 The crushed pain receptors let in a chemical released from the injured areas. This kick-starts a nerve signal that blasts up to your brain.

4 The deeper the pain receptors the less sensitive they are – that's why a really bad injury can hurt less than a little scratch.

splinter

ARGH!

OOPS!!

SWOOSH!

5 Different pain signals move at different speeds. A sharp prick on your skin hits your brain at 30 metres per second. A longer pulse like a burning or aching pain moves through the neurons at a more leisurely 2 metres per second.

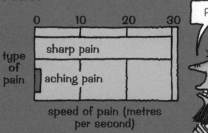

FASCINATING!

type of pain	0	10	20	30
sharp pain				
aching pain				

speed of pain (metres per second)

HORRIBLE HEARING

Ears are eerie things. After all, just think how odd some people's ears look. And guess what? They're even odder on the inside!

WHAT'RE YOU STARING AT?

4. The semi-circular canals. Scientists use the word 'canal' to mean any long thin space in the body. Like a carpenter's level, the canals are full of liquid that sloshes around as your head moves. Sensors in the canals stop you losing your balance. This is good news for tight-rope walkers!

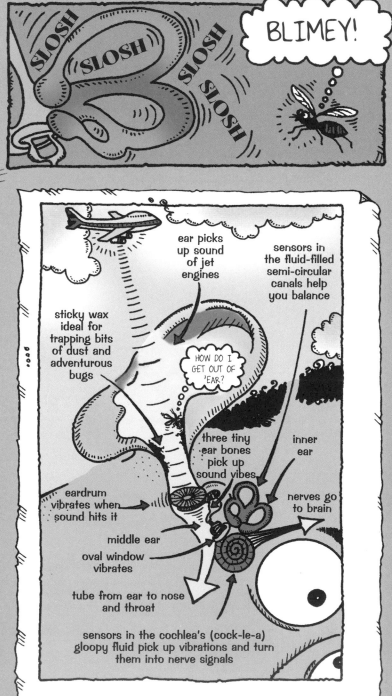

SLOSH SLOSH SLOSH SLOSH

BLIMEY!

The ears work like a couple of satellite dishes linked up to a drum, linked up to a triangle and stick, linked to a microphone with a carpenter's level attached! Simple, isn't it? Your ears pick up sound signals in the air and bounce them into a central hole.

Imagine a wandering ugly bug, say a fly, sneaking into the ear. Here's what it would see...

1. The external ear canal (that's yer ear 'ole).

YUCK! STICKY WAX!

ZOOM

2. The eardrum. It trembles when sounds hit it.

CRIKEY, A GIANT DRUM!

SHAKE RATTLE BUZZ

3. Meanwhile, in the middle ear, three tiny ear bones are doing their castanets impression by passing on the fly's irritating buzz.They jangle like a triangle hit by a stick.

anvil bone

stirrup bone

BUZZ

hammer bone

hammer

anvil

stirrup

ear picks up sound of jet engines

sensors in the fluid-filled semi-circular canals help you balance

sticky wax ideal for trapping bits of dust and adventurous bugs

HOW DO I GET OUT OF 'EAR?

three tiny ear bones pick up sound vibes

inner ear

eardrum vibrates when sound hits it

nerves go to brain

middle ear

oval window vibrates

tube from ear to nose and throat

sensors in the cochlea's (cock-le-a) gloopy fluid pick up vibrations and turn them into nerve signals

5. The cochlea picks up the sounds and makes them into nerve signals that go to the brain. It's like a microphone picking up sounds and sending them down a wire.

COCHLEA – HMM, THAT MEANS SNAIL IN LATIN!

6. That fly's a genius. That's where the name comes from. And now the nerves are buzzing with sound messages for the brain.

THIS IS GETTING ON MY NERVES – I'M OUT OF HERE

URGENT HORRIBLE HEALTH WARNING!

Dear Reader,

Are you reading this page in a car or a ship? Well – DON'T. If you try to concentrate on something that keeps moving your semi-circular canals end up getting confused. Your brain is baffled by the confusing signals and (according to one theory) produces chemicals that make you violently sick!

Could you be a sound scientist?

Try to predict the result of this sound experiment. If you get it right you'll certainly have something to shout about. Scientists have discovered that our hearing is sharpest for sounds of a certain frequency. Which sounds do we hear most clearly?

a) Loud music.

b) A coin dropping on the floor.

c) A teacher talking.

Scientists have found that the ear is most sensitive to sounds at 500–3000Hz – that's the level of a person talking. So sad but true: the answer above is **c)** a teacher talking.

Dare you discover...
why your ears go POP?

All you do is:

1. Yawn deeply and listen to yourself.

2. You may hear a few tiny tingling pops at the start of the yawn.

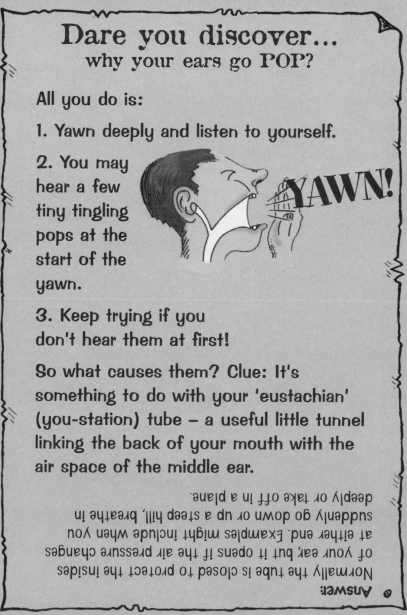

YAWN!

3. Keep trying if you don't hear them at first!

So what causes them? Clue: It's something to do with your 'eustachian' (you-station) tube – a useful little tunnel linking the back of your mouth with the air space of the middle ear.

Answer: Normally the tube is closed to protect the insides of your ear, but it opens if the air pressure changes at either end. Examples might include when you suddenly go down or up a steep hill, breathe in deeply or take off in a plane.

ODDBALL EYEBALL

You peel open your lids, rub sleepy dust from your eyes and stare at… EEK! A spider has dropped in to check you out. So what exactly is going on inside your eyeball?

1. Six muscles hold your eyeball in place and contract or relax to allow your eye to swivel in the direction of the spider.

2. Light rays from the spider pass through your cornea – the eye's curved 'front window' that starts the process of focusing the image.

3. It goes through the pupil, which is a black hole surrounded by the iris – the colourful bit of your eye (**3a**). This wheel of muscles (**3b**) tightens or relaxes to let more or less light into your eye.

4. Behind the pupil is the lens – a transparent, squishy disk that gets slimmer or fatter as it focuses on whatever you're looking at, far or near.

5. When the light rays from the spider hit the back of your eye, the retina, they fall on millions of cells called rods and cones. The cones (**5a**) detect colours and only work in bright light, while the rods (**5b**) see in shades of black, white or grey and only work in dim light.

6. The image is converted into electrical messages and relayed by nerve cells along the optic nerve (**6a**) to the brain (**6b**).

7. Notice how the image of the spider on the back of they eye is upside down? This happened as the light waves passed through the lens. Luckily your brilliant brain is a super–computer – it knows to flip the image it receives from the eye the right way up.

8. For all this action to take place, your eye needs to be supplied with oxygen. It arrives on tiny red blood cells in your blood, through arteries (**8b**). The cells are then carried in veins (**8b**) back to the lungs to pick up fresh oxygen before the heart whooshes them round once again.

TASTY OR SMELLY?

You will need:

- a blindfold
- paper and a pencil
- a friend
- small plastic cups of orange, apple and pineapple juice
- a small slice of apple
- a small slice of raw onion
- slightly mashed banana
- some mashed potato
- some crumbly cheese
- a slice of pickled beetroot
- a slice of tinned peaches
- a spoonful of baked beans
- a spoonful of green peas

Do you trust your senses of taste and smell? Maybe you do, but without the other senses working with them, then you might find some unexpected results!

HORRIBLE HEALTH WARNING!
Get help from an adult cutting up food. Also check with them that you don't have any allergies to anything in the experiment.

1 In all the experiments you can swap with your friend who does the tasting and who puts out the food. The one tasting must wear the blindfold or shut their eyes, and hold their nose at the same time.

2 The first experiment. Take the plastic cups of apple, orange and pineapple juice, swap them round, and guide your pal to taste them. Make them hold their nose and write down their guesses for each taste.

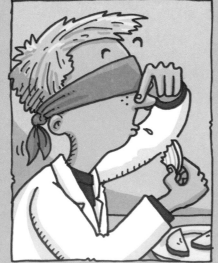

3 Did they get it right? Now you have a go with the slice of apple and raw onion. If you can't see or smell them, it's hard to taste which is which! Amazing!

4 Now the cheese, mashed potato and banana. See how tricky it is to taste when you're holding your nose. Let your friend try too, and swap food around.

5 Next, test your pal with the tinned peaches and the pickled beetroot. Make sure your friend doesn't know which is which. With the texture so similar, can they taste the difference without sight and smell?

6 Finally, see if you can tell the difference between the baked beans and peas. It might be tricky. But eat too many and you'll soon find some of their other interesting side-effects!

Go to page 60 to discover the science secret behind this experiment.

Reckless Reflexes

Remember, reflexes are moves you make without thinking, so which of these **AREN'T** reflexes?

1. Snatching your hand away from heat

OW!

2. Blinking

BLINK! *BLINK!*

3. Riding a bicycle

WOBBLE! *WOBBLE!*

4. Sneezing

ATISHOO!

5. Getting washed in the morning

SPLISH! *SPLASH!* *SPLOSH!*

6. Hair standing on end when scared

YIKES!

7. Rolling your eyes

ROLL! *ROLL!*

8. Eating breakfast

SCOFF!

Twitchy Wordsearch

Can you find the 12 sensitive words hidden in this grid?

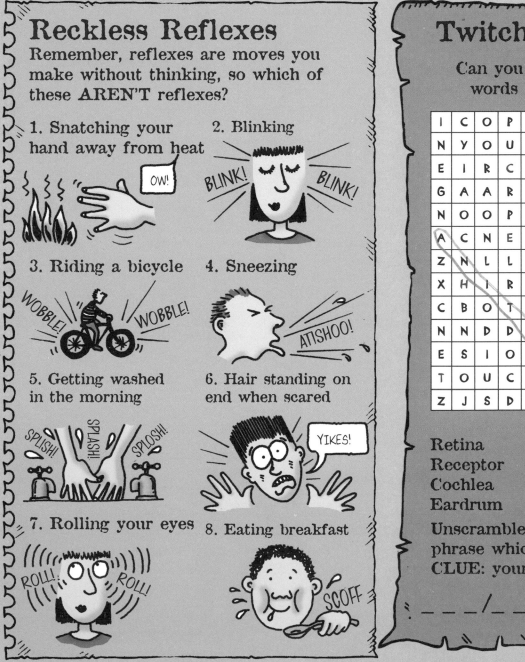

I	C	O	P	E	Y	A	T	N	L	L	O	M
N	Y	O	U	U	E	X	I	A	L	H	N	S
E	I	R	C	N	O	A	J	S	S	O	Q	L
G	A	A	R	H	R	E	C	E	P	T	O	R
N	O	O	P	A	L	N	B	V	K	V	E	C
A	C	N	E	I	E	E	D	R	H	S	L	O
Z	N	L	L	U	K	D	A	E	E	A	E	N
X	H	I	R	X	E	U	Z	N	A	C	O	E
C	B	O	T	Y	H	C	U	O	R	G	F	S
N	N	D	D	E	W	A	O	T	D	P	K	D
E	S	I	O	X	R	A	B	U	R	D	A	C
T	O	U	C	H	P	F	L	A	U	N	S	K
Z	J	S	D	O	R	F	B	D	M	Z	H	G

Retina   Cornea   Cones
Receptor   Neuron   Touch
Cochlea   Pain   Nerves
Eardrum   Rods   Taste

Unscramble the red letters to find a phrase which means 'the best'.
CLUE: your moggy has them.

_ _ _ _ / _ _ _ ' _ / _ _ _ _ _ _ _

Turn to page 60 to see the answers.

FOUL FOOD AND DIGESTION

Inside every one of us there's a fabulously foul food processing factory, and it's on the go non-stop, turning meals into energy for our brains and bodies.

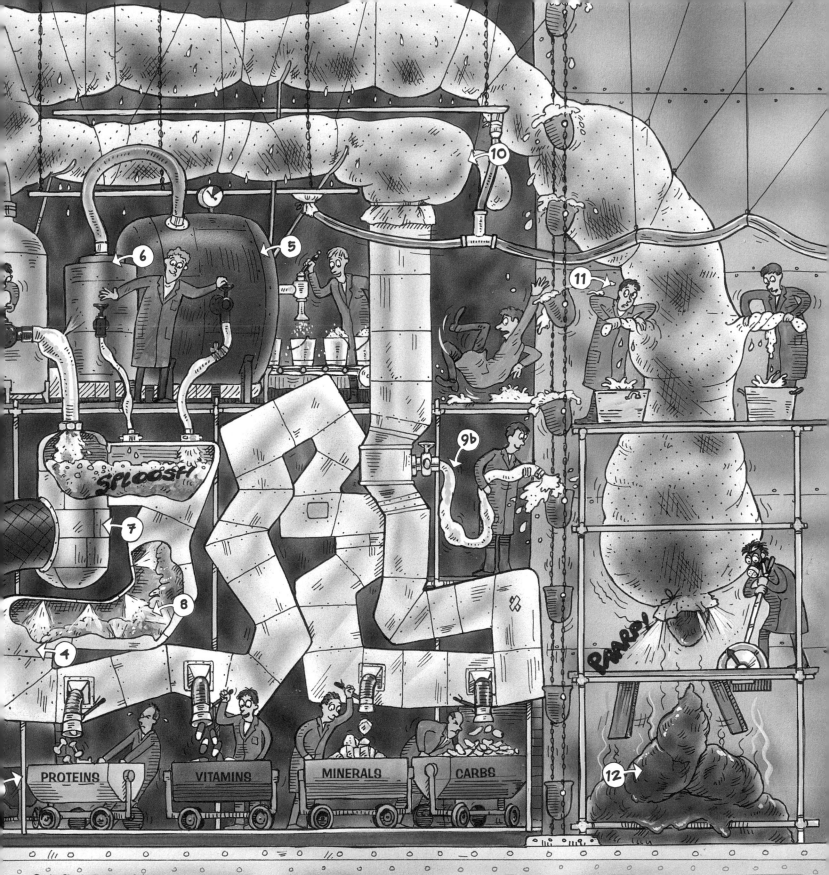

GUTSY PERFORMANCE

Digestion begins in the mouth **(1)** where food is ground up by the teeth, squished by the tongue and mixed with saliva. It slides down the throat into a tube called the gullet **(2)** where it becomes a ball of goo called a bolus. The gullet's squeezing action forces it down into the stomach **(3)** where stomach juices turn it into a mush called chyme. Then it's on to the small intestine **(4)** where bile from the liver **(5)** powerful enzymes from the pancreas **(6)** salty juices from the duodenum **(7)** and slime from the intestine walls **(8)** turn the chyme into mushy soup while the body takes what it needs in the form of vitamins, carbohydrates, proteins and minerals **(9a)** and fat **(9b)**. What's left moves into the large intestine **(10)**. Most of the water is taken back into the body in the first bit of the colon **(11)** leaving sticky poo to get squeezed out as whiffy waste at the other end **(12)**.

TUMMY TROUBLE

Stomach churning? Guts clenching? Chances are some beastly bacteria have invaded your belly and made you ill. But not all bacteria are bad – as abdominal adventurer Wanda Wye is about to discover…

WANDA'S JUST SPLASH-LANDED IN THE STOMACH - YOUR BEASTLY BODY'S FOOD STORAGE TANK.

INTESTINES THIS WAY

I'M NOT SURE I'VE GOT THE STOMACH FOR THIS…

PLOP!

IT'S TIME FOR OUR INTREPID EXPLORER TO TAKE THE PLUNGE…

IT'S NOT LONG BEFORE WANDA SPOTS THE SCOURGE OF ALL STOMACHS - SALMONELLA. THIS MEAN MICROBE'S RESPONSIBLE FOR GRINDING THE GUTS OF MORE THAN A MILLION PEOPLE EVERY SINGLE YEAR.

NEXT TO BE CAUGHT BY WANDA'S BEAM IS ANOTHER BAD BACTERIA - LISTERIA. IT'S FAIRLY RARE BUT IF IT DOES MANAGE TO SNEAK INTO YOUR STOMACH YOU'LL SOON BE FEELING FOUL.

IT'S NOT THE FRIENDLIEST OF BACTERIA…

GET OUT OF MY WAY!

GROAN!

FIVE SECONDS ON THE FLOOR - THAT'S ALL IT TOOK FOR HER TO GET A GRIP.

TEE HEE! READY FOR A ROLLER-COASTER RIDE? IT'S GONNA BE EXPLOSIVE!

CHURN

THIS BODY OWNER'S GOING TO BE GUTTED.

WANDA'S SURFACED IN THE SMALL INTESTINE AND HER LUCK'S IN - SHE'S COME ACROSS A HUGE COLONY OF 'GOOD' BACTERIA.

YOUR GUTS ARE HOME TO UP TO ONE THOUSAND DIFFERENT TYPES OF BACTERIA. MANY OF THEM HELP YOU STAY HEALTHY. HERE'S WHAT SCIENTISTS HAVE DISCOVERED THEY CAN DO:

WE'RE NOT ALL BAD!

CAN I HELP YOU?

CHOMP!

TUCK IN!

IT'S A BIT CHEWY…

HELLO! PLEASED TO MEET YOU!

IT'S GOOD TO SEE SOME FRIENDLY FACES!

SOME 'FRIENDLY' BACTERIA EAT THE BITS OF FOOD THAT YOU CAN'T DIGEST AND TURN IT INTO SUGARS THAT YOUR BODY CAN USE FOR ENERGY.

A HORRIBLY HEALTHY DIET

**Just like a car needs petrol, you need food. Without it, you'd come to a stop…
and shortly after a full stop! But how do you know which foods will keep you
running like a limo rather than spluttering like a junkheap? Read on…**

There's a lot more to food than meets the eye. There are loads of vital ingredients that you must have in your daily diet. To find out more we persuaded our Private Eye MI Gutzache to sneak into the school kitchens to collect samples…

Gutzache investigates

It was time for the protective suit. And I insisted on a gas mask… these particular samples smelled ancient. I figured they could be emetic (that's something that makes you sick as a dog)!

SAMPLE 1 – SCHOOL DINNER POTATO
This sad potato was about to be boiled, but was still a healthy specimen. This is what I found hiding in it:

- One slug*
- 81% water
- 0.4% protein
- 16% carbohydrate (in the form of starch)
- 0.1% fat
- 0.8% fibre
- 0.7% vitamins
- 1% minerals

HI!

NOTES
The slug had no complaints

* The slug also contained these ingredients but in different amounts. At least this time it didn't get cooked with the potato!

SAMPLE 2 – SCHOOL DINNER CHIPS
The chips were cold, greasy and oozing with fat. The fats stay around longer than most foods and at least they make you feel full. But spare fat turns into body fat, slopping around your belly and bum.

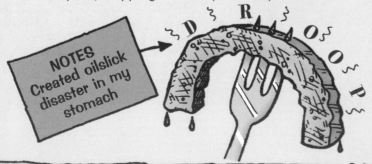

NOTES
Created oilslick disaster in my stomach

SAMPLE 3 – JAM PUDDING
This pud is oozing with sticky sugar. Sugar gives your body energy but there's already enough sugar inside me to fill a jam jar.

NOTES
Just looking at it gave me toothache

SAMPLE 4 – MASHED SWEDE
Hidden in this weird lump of orange vegetable I found a tasteless food chemical called starch – a type of carbohydrate, the same as in potato. It's made of sugar chemicals joined in a chain. Inside your muscles enzymes can rip apart these sugars and free the energy to help your body move.

SAMPLE 5 – SMELLY CHEESE

NOTES
Relieved to find the smell wasn't from my socks

GHASTLY PONG

Cheese is 25% protein – your body uses this to build muscles. Your body is 20% protein but you don't need to eat tonnes of it. If you're 12 years old you need about 55 grams of protein a day. Protein also hangs out in milk, fish, meat, beans and nuts.

NOTES
I've sketched some useful sources of protein

SAMPLE 6 – SCHOOL PRUNES

Can't say I liked the taste and they had a weird leathery texture. But my investigation showed that's 'cos they're loaded with fibre. That's the stuff that makes brown bread chewy and fruit and veg stringy. Seems your body can't digest fibre but it keeps the rest of your food moving in the gut. The gut walls can grip the fibre more easily than ordinary food. In the end this gets you moving, too... to the bathroom.

NOTES Useful for washing taste of dinner away

stray pea

greasy finger prints

SAMPLE 7 – GLASS OF WATER

It wasn't much to look at, but I found you need about two litres of this clear runny stuff every day. Half comes from water in your food (like the potato), and half from what you drink. You must top up your water supply 'cos your body is 66% water and bits such as your brain are 80% water. Guess what'll happen if you don't drink enough of it? Pea-brain!

Mysterious minerals

So, from what MI Gutzache has discovered, eat lots of different foods and you'll get everything your body needs to stay healthy. Brilliant! But what happens if you are a vegetarian and don't eat meat or fish? Or if you're vegan and don't eat meat, fish or any foods made by animals, such as milk and eggs? Either way, it's fine as long as you get the vitamins and minerals you need.

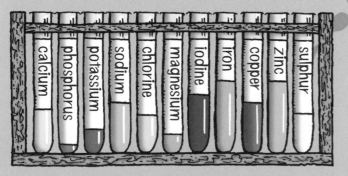

calcium | phosphorus | potassium | sodium | chlorine | magnesium | iodine | iron | copper | zinc | sulphur

The school dinner samples were loaded with these mysterious minerals. They're vital in tiny amounts for building your body and making useful chemicals.

Bet you never knew!

Sugar hangs out in loads of savoury foods, too – a small tin of baked beans contains two to three teaspoons of sugar. You'll find it in cereals, tinned meat, soup, tinned vegetables, peanut butter and even coleslaw. Sweet foods have even more sugar – a chocolate bar has ten teaspoonfuls. Most of us probably get through 30 teaspoons of sugar a day!

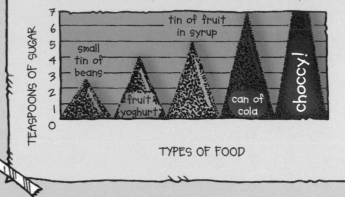

TEASPOONS OF SUGAR

small tin of beans
fruit yoghurt
tin of fruit in syrup
can of cola
choccy!

TYPES OF FOOD

A disgustingly unhealthy diet

If you eat just a very few things you won't get all the vital goodies. The most disgusting diet of all is not to eat anything. Surprise! Food is good for you, hunger is bad for you. Scientists have found that children who miss breakfast find it hard to learn new things at school. Don't try this excuse. And just look what happens to a really starving body…

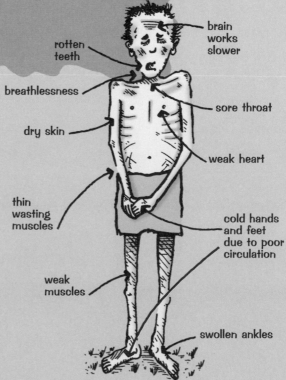

rotten teeth

brain works slower

breathlessness

sore throat

dry skin

weak heart

thin wasting muscles

cold hands and feet due to poor circulation

weak muscles

swollen ankles

INTERNATIONAL SANDWICH!

Made from specialist foods from around the world, open wide for the ultimate horrible sandwich. Feeling hungry?

1. Italian spaghetti contains carbohydrate for energy.

2. Scottish beef and haggis — both full of B vitamins and protein. The haggis may be fatty!

3. German sausage is vitamin B-rich, but also has fat!

4. Greek olives are full of vitamin E for muscles and skin.

5. Welsh leeks contain vitamin C, little fat, but can make you fart!

6. English lettuce contains vitamin C; carrots contain vitamin A.

7. The French like salted, boiled snails — they're full of protein!

8. Spanish sardines are rich in calcium for strong teeth and bones, as is Icelandic cod (**8a**).

9. Chinese stir-fried vegetables — bamboo shoots, and spinach, are good for your blood. Prawns are protein-rich.

10. Dutch Edam cheese gives you protein but also lots of fat.

11. Danish bacon is a good source of iron for blood. Beware of fat!

12. American fried chicken is full of protein. Deep fried is bad for you!

13. Indian 'curries' are a popular takeaway. Oily ones can be fatty.

14. Australians sometimes eat protein-packed kangaroo meat.

15. Canada produces lots of wheat for the bun which contains niacin, a B-vitamin.

16. South African dried-meat biltong is high in protein and low in fat!

17. Japanese boiled wasp larvae, and fried grasshoppers are nutritious, as is the Nigerian kanni (**17a**), a boiled caterpillar. Mmm!

18. The fries include Irish potatoes, a source of carbohydrate. Look out for fat!

19. The milkshake contains Costa Rican bananas which are packed with energy and vitamins.

OOZE!

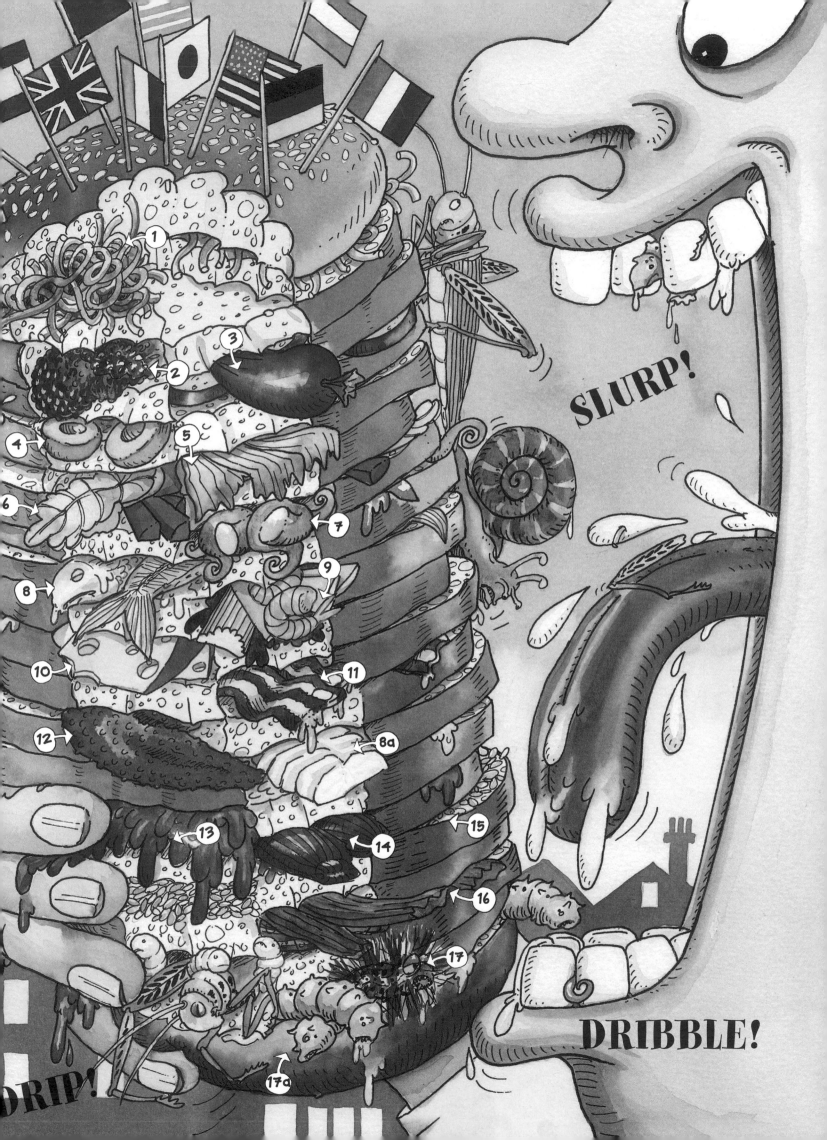

MAKE YOUR OWN
EDIBLE EYEBALLS

You will need:

- 25g Rice Krispies
- 75g milk chocolate
- 8 tbsp icing sugar
- giant Smarties
- black writing icing
- clingfilm
- saucepan
- bowl to fit over saucepan
- mixing bowl
- mixing spoon
- teaspoon

WARNING!
Cooking can be dangerous. MAKE SURE you get an adult to help with the panel marked with this sign.

Fancy cooking up something that's as delicious as it's revolting? How about crunchy chocolate eyeballs?

MELT
POUR

1 Break up the chocolate and melt it in a bowl over a saucepan of boiling water. Mix the Rice Krispies into the melted chocolate and leave to cool.

TWIST

2 Cut small squares of clingfilm and put a heaped teaspoonful of the mix on to each square. Shape into a ball, twist the ends together to secure and leave in the fridge to harden.

SPLODGE!

3 Put the icing sugar in a bowl and mix with hot water to make a thick paste. When cool, remove the clingfilm and coat the eyeballs with the icing.

GRRRR!

4 Stick a Smartie onto each eyeball and add a large black dot of writing icing as a pupil.

Feeling Foul

Using bits of yucky-textured food, tell your friends you've hidden imitation body bits in boxes. See what gut-wrenching ideas they come up with when they use only their fingers to squidge them around...

You will need:

- 5 shoeboxes with lids
- scissors
- 5 small bowls
- 2 peeled cherry tomatoes
- 4 or 5 pieces of popcorn
- 2 cold scrambled eggs
- 2 cold cooked sausages
- a small piece of clingfilm coated with cooking oil

1 Cut a hole in the lid of each shoebox, big enough to get your hand through. Put tomatoes, clingfilm, eggs, sausages and popcorn in separate bowls and put each inside a shoebox. Replace lids.

DROOL!

YUCK!

Go to the Puzzle answers on page 60 to find out what your friends should think they're feeling!.

2 Ask your friends to try and guess what the various body parts are just by feeling them. (Wash hands afterwards and don't eat the foods.)

SPOT THE DIFFERENCE

Can you spot the six differences in the pictures below?

Wicked Wordsearch

See how sharp-eyed you are by finding the 12 words below. Watch out, the words can go forwards and backwards!

G	J	H	T	L	M	N	P	X	I	P	M	K
T	A	S	C	U	I	A	N	D	N	C	U	D
Y	E	L	T	A	N	V	E	E	T	O	N	P
T	I	C	L	C	M	N	E	B	E	L	U	V
V	E	Q	R	B	U	O	Z	R	S	O	J	Y
R	I	E	D	M	L	W	T	F	T	N	E	P
V	A	X	Z	V	R	A	I	S	I	C	J	A
S	M	O	U	T	H	E	D	M	N	N	J	N
M	U	E	L	I	Y	A	C	D	E	A	E	Y
L	L	A	I	O	M	V	M	T	E	P	J	M
H	G	N	T	U	C	O	I	U	M	R	W	E
D	B	I	L	E	F	U	T	L	M	T	O	J
M	U	N	E	D	O	U	D	S	L	I	A	R

Bile	Ileum	Mouth
Colon	Intestine	Pancreas
Duodenum	Jejunum	Rectum
Gallbladder	Liver	Stomach

Turn to page 60 to see the answers.

39

STAGGERING STOMACH

After chomping down a big meal, your food ends up in this stretchy sac getting churned up into a mushy pulp known as chyme.

STAGGERING STOMACH FACT FILE

NAME: Stomach

THE BASIC FACTS: The stomach is a storage tank for food. Its job is to mix and squash food to make it easier to digest. Food stays there from 1.5 to 4.5 hours depending on what you've eaten and how much.

THE HORRIBLE DETAILS: There's a type of germ that lives in the stomach eating your half-digested food.

SPLOSH

SQUELZ

GLUG GLUG

GRRRGH!

WHOOSH

SQUELZ

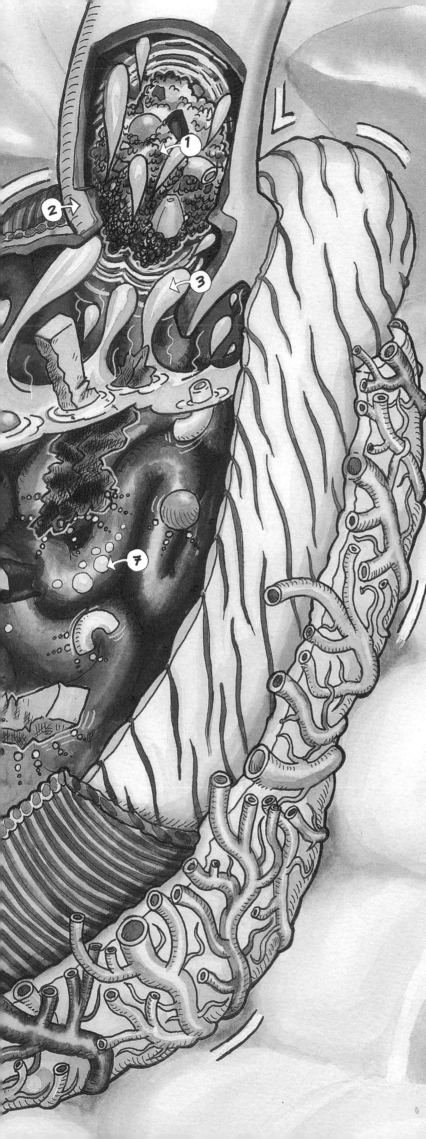

THAT FED-UP FEELING...

1. Ball of mushed-up food that's swallowed and passed to your stomach. It's called a bolus.

2. Ring of muscle that opens and then contracts to let the bolus into the stomach.

3. Stomach juice sometimes goes back up the oesophagus – that's the tube from your mouth to your stomach. This can happen when you're exercising or if you bend down after wolfing down a big meal. The acid in the juice burns the lining of the oesophagus, giving you an uncomfortable burning sensation.

4. Folds in the stomach lining enable the stomach to expand when you've just scoffed a huge meal. Scientists call these folds rugae (say roo-guy).

5. Stomach juice starts to digest your food.

6. Slimy goo, called mucus, oozes out of the stomach lining and protects the stomach against the acid in the stomach juices and stops the stomach digesting itself!

7. Swallowed air, taken in while scoffing. The rumbling sound from your stomach is caused by these air bubbles and your stomach juice churning together.

8. Meat is tough to digest and hangs out in your stomach for hours.

9. Live yoghurt is much kinder as it contains friendly bacteria that can live quite happily in the guts and even aid digestion.

10. Some food, such as sweetcorn, doesn't always get broken down into chyme and passes right through you!

11. Layers of muscle in the stomach churn up your food into a mush called chyme.

12. Ring of muscle that lets the chyme pass from the stomach into the small intestine.

HORRIBLE HEALTHCARE

Your body is designed to last a lifetime but Baron Frankenstein's monster needs a rotten refit…

1. The Baron's radical robot doctors insert brand new muscle blocks, and sew them up tight!

2. When joints begin to wear, the cartilage (rubbery gristle) that cushions the bone ends becomes thin and begins to rub, producing a ghastly range of clicks, pops and squeaks. A service robot oils the monster's knees.

3. Another robot doctor studies X-rays of the monster's body. It looks like he's already had a knock-up kneecap replacement (**3a**) and a halfcocked hip op (**3b**).

4. The radical refit continues with a new liver and kidneys – which all sounds pretty offal!

5. Running-repair robots patch the monster's 'crust' with 'slices' of artificial skin (**5a**).

6. The monster's getting a transfusion of new blood. Fresh red blood cells will help carry more oxygen to the monster's muscles.

7. A service robot readies his dentist's drill and prepares to deliver a new set of dentures.

8. The Baron makes sure his monster has 20-20 vision with corrective laser eye surgery (**8a**).

9. One robot cleans ears and fits a cochlear implant – a super hearing aid connected to the brain (**9a**)…

10. …while another fits a pacemaker to a new heart – how heartening! Soon the monster will be ticking along nicely!

HORRID HEALTHCHECK

Doctors and nurses have lots of high-tech tests for finding out how fit you are. But just taking a closer look at your body can tell them a lot too…

HERE'S PAUL, PROUD OWNER OF ONE PARTICULARLY BEASTLY BODY.

HELLO HANDSOME!

STOP POSING SONNY, I HAVEN'T GOT ALL DAY.

PAUL'S GETTING READY TO GIVE HIMSELF A HORRIBLE HEALTHCHECK. GRUMPY DR GRIMGRAVE IS HERE TO HELP OUT BY SCORING EACH TEST OUT OF TEN.

NOW TAKE A DEEP BREATH AND EXHALE…

UGGGHHH!

AAAAAH!

WHIFF!

LET'S START BY TAKING A LOOK AT PAUL'S TONGUE.

BLAH!

BLEAUGH!

IN TRADITIONAL CHINESE MEDICINE, IT'S THOUGHT THAT THE STATE OF THE SURFACE OF YOUR TONGUE CAN PROVIDE CLUES TO CONDITIONS IN OTHER PARTS OF THE BODY.

PAUL'S TERRIFICALLY LONG TONGUE IS PINK WITH A LIGHT FURRY COATING - LOOKING PRETTY GOOD, PAUL!

THE SURFACE COULD DO WITH A SCRAPE BUT IT'S OTHERWISE OK. I'LL GIVE THIS FASCINATING MOUTH MUSCLE NINE OUT OF TEN.

IF THE TONGUE'S TOO PALE OR TOO DARK IT MIGHT BE A SIGN THAT ITS OWNER ISN'T GETTING ENOUGH VITAMINS. A VERY FURRY TONGUE MAY BE A SIGN OF A FUNGAL INFECTION AND A SWOLLEN TONGUE COULD BE A SYMPTOM OF SOMETHING MORE SERIOUS.

BAD BREATH MAY BE A SIGN OF MOUTH AND TOOTH TROUBLE. MOST PONGY BREATH PROBLEMS ARE CAUSED BY A BUILD-UP OF BACTERIA ON YOUR TONGUE BUT IN THIS CASE IT'S PAUL'S TEETH THAT NEED SOME TLC.

HE COULD DO WITH BRUSHING-UP ON HIS DENTAL HYGIENE.

PAUL'S HONKING HALITOSIS* EARNS HIM JUST FOUR POINTS FROM GRUMPY GRIMGRAVE.

*HALITOSIS (HAL-I-TOE-SIS) IS THE MEDICAL NAME FOR CHRONIC BAD BREATH.

NEXT STOP IS THE EYE WHERE DR GRIMGRAVE IS CONDUCTING A CLOSE-UP INSPECTION.

EYE-SPY...

HE NEEDS TO TAKE MORE BREAKS FROM HIS COMPUTER GAMES - STARING AT THE SCREEN'S DRYING HIS EYES OUT. EIGHT POINTS - AND TWO MORE TESTS TO GO!

BLOODSHOT EYES CAN BE CAUSED BY ALL SORTS OF THINGS INCLUDING ALLERGIES, INFECTIONS - AND INVADING INSECTS! YELLOW EYES ARE USUALLY LINKED TO LIVER PROBLEMS.

THE WHITES OF PAUL'S PEEPERS ARE A BIT BLOODSHOT BUT THE DOC DOESN'T THINK IT'S ANYTHING TO WORRY ABOUT.

GRIMGRAVE'S LAST TWO TESTS INVOLVE EXAMINING THE WASTE PRODUCTS OF PAUL'S BEASTLY BODY. MODERN DOCTORS RARELY DO THIS - IT'S NOT A JOB FOR THE FAINT-HEARTED...

WE'LL LET HIM SQUEEZE OUT HIS SAMPLES IN PRIVATE.

PLOP!

THE COLOUR OF YOUR PEE WILL TELL YOU WHETHER YOU'RE DRINKING ENOUGH WATER. IT'S USUALLY PALE YELLOW BUT WILL BE DARKER IF YOU'RE DEHYDRATED.

HMM, FASCINATING - THIS PATIENT'S URINE (AS WE DOCTORS CALL IT) IS DEEP YELLOW AND STRONG-SMELLING. THIS SHOWS LOW FLUID INTAKE AND SCORES JUST FIVE POINTS.

IF YOUR PEE IS CLOUDY IT COULD MEAN YOU HAVE AN INFECTION. DOCTORS CAN ALSO USE A DIPSTICK TO DIAGNOSE A DISEASE CALLED DIABETES*.

*DIABETES (DIE-AH-BEE-TEES) IS A DISEASE THAT CAUSES THE BODY TO HAVE HIGH LEVELS OF SUGAR IN THE BLOOD.

LAST BUT NOT LEAST, IT'S TIME FOR DR GRIMGRAVE TO TAKE A PEEK AT PAUL'S POO. HE CHECKS THE CHUNKS AGAINST HIS CHART.

PAUL'S PASSED HIS HORRID HEALTHCHECK WITH AN AVERAGE SCORE OF SEVEN OUT OF TEN. IF HE TAKES THE DOC'S ADVICE HE'LL PASS THE NEXT ONE WITH FLYING COLOURS.

SOFT, SMOOTH AND SAUSAGE-LIKE - PAUL'S PRODUCED THE PERFECT POO. TEN OUT OF TEN!

PONG!

PAUL'S POO IS A HEALTHY BROWN COLOUR. AN UNUSUAL DIET OR DISEASE CAN RESULT IN OTHER COLOURS.

REMEMBER, IF YOU THINK THERE MIGHT BE SOMETHING WRONG WITH YOUR BEASTLY BODY, DON'T RELY ON YOUR OWN DIAGNOSIS - GO AND SEE A DOCTOR.

AS I TELL MY IDIOT PATIENTS - LOOK AFTER YOUR BODY AND IT WILL LOOK AFTER YOU.

FANTASTIC PHYSIQUE

We all own an amazing and unique piece of machinery, a marvel of natural engineering. Here's what an ad for your body might look like…

1. The body has a super-stretchy, germ-proof, wrap-around coating (known as skin) that protects the body bits inside. Its built-in self-cooling system (**1a**) known as sweat, oozes from holes in the skin (called pores) when the body is too hot. In cold temperatures, hairs sticking out of the skin stand on end, trapping pockets of warm air between them as insulation. If the skin is damaged, it has a self-repair system. First the body's state-of-the-art fluid transport system, also called the blood supply (**1b**), squirts blood out to clean the wound. Then it releases a clotting agent to create a plug, called a scab (**1c**), over the hole while skin grows back underneath.

2. The thermal head-covering known to body owners as hair is made up of about 100,000 individual hairs (older models may have less) and comes in a variety of colours (**2a**).

3. Head hair keeps the body's amazing info processing unit (the brain) warm. To function properly, it needs to be warmer than the rest of the body. It also needs 20 per cent of all the body's energy supply, which for its size is 10 times more than nearly all other bits.

4. Fuel is kept in a storage tank (called the stomach) and broken down in the guts into chemicals to power the body.

5. The body's super-strong support framework (called the skeleton). It stops the body flopping to the floor and is made of 206 calcium and phosphate bits, called bones.

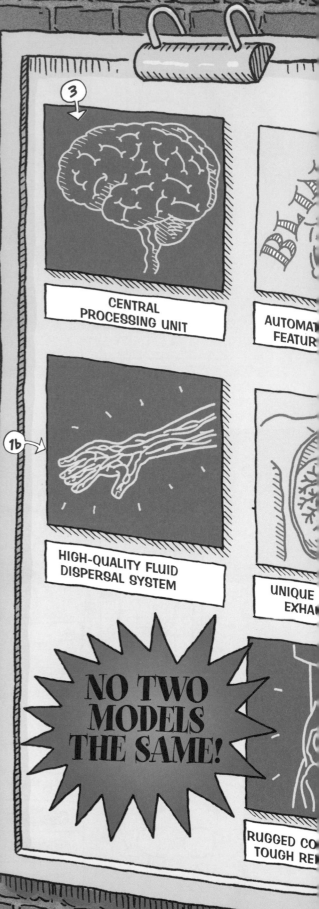

CENTRAL PROCESSING UNIT

AUTOMAT FEATUR

HIGH-QUALITY FLUID DISPERSAL SYSTEM

UNIQUE EXHA

NO TWO MODELS THE SAME!

RUGGED CO TOUGH RE

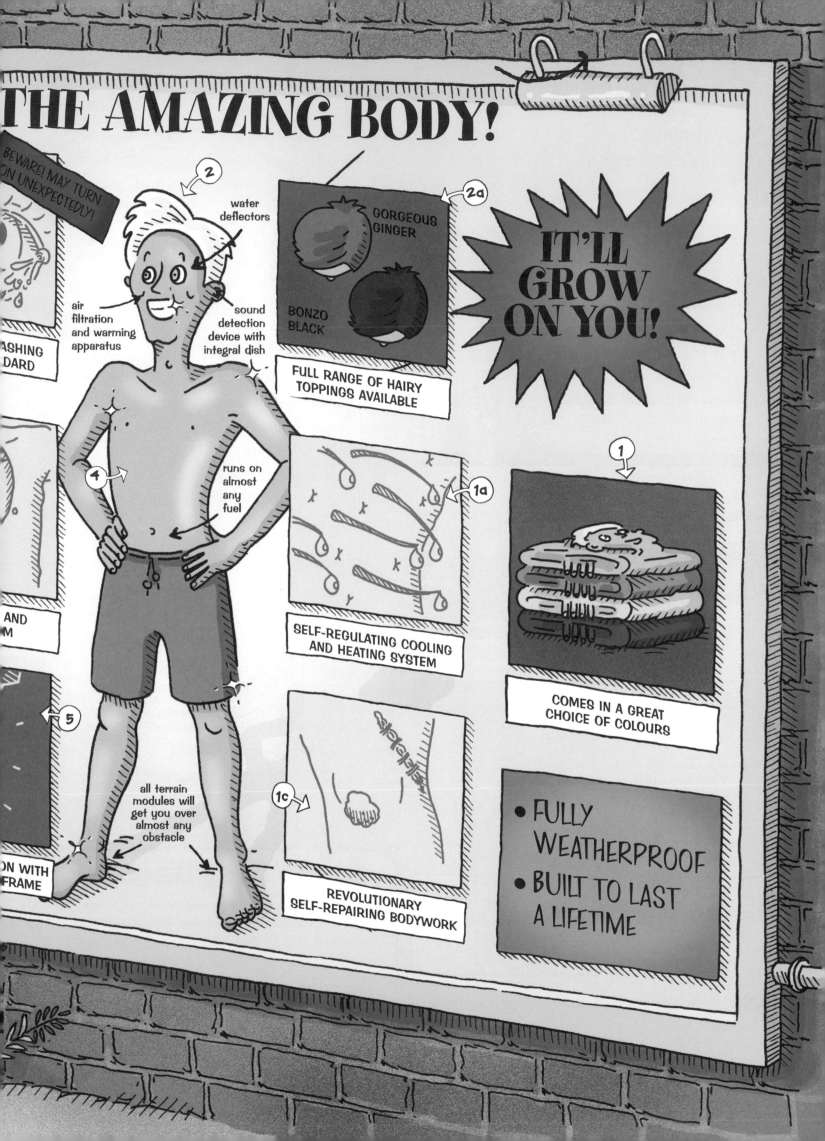

BEASTLY BODY CARE

SQUEEZE!

Warning! You've got to look after your body properly. If it breaks down, you'll find getting hold of a new body is harder than juggling custard. So you really do need a body-care routine.

Listen up! It's morning already… Your body is programmed to wake up automatically at roughly the same time each day. The brain senses the light falling on the eyelids and switches to full-power mode as the light becomes brighter. Try stretching your body to test its muscle motor power units.

I ALWAYS WAKE THE MONSTER BRIGHT AND EARLY…

RISE AND SHINE - IT'S NEARLY MIDNIGHT!

GROAN!

…followed by a body stretch!

WHIMPER!

Unlike humans, the Monster needs a powerful electric shock to wake him…

IT'S FOR YOUR OWN GOOD, MONSTER!

SQUEEZE!

The toilet shuffle

Once your body is awake it has to be shuffled to the toilet to commence the liquid waste expulsion procedure known as peeing. Human bodies are designed to squirt out unwanted pee at regular intervals and your body will have a full bladder store of pee from the night.

WIDDLE

CLOSE THE DOOR!

The bladder sends nerve signals to the brain as it stretches and fills up with pee. It's a good idea to let the body pee before the bladder gets too full, otherwise it could leak embarrassingly.

All-over body cleaning

Older body owners give their bodies at least a daily bath or shower. But young owners may think NEVER is often enough!

It's certainly useful to wash unwanted germs and sweat from the skin using soap and water. But soap stings the eyes and in the morning you should use a clean damp cloth to gently wipe sleepy dust from this sensitive region.

After all-over body cleaning, dry between your toes so athlete's foot fungus won't grow and damage the skin.

CLEAN BEHIND YOUR EARS OR I'LL GIVE THEM TO SOMEBODY ELSE

ATHLETE'S FOOT WITHOUT ATHLETE'S FOOT

MONSTER'S FOOT WITH ATHLETE'S FOOT

Hair-cleaning routine

A body-cleaning session is a good time to wash your hair. Afterwards, wet hair can be separated and smoothed down using a brush.

Dead Disgusting

Body owners should not copy women in Nepal, who traditionally wash their husband's disgustingly dirty feet and DRINK the water. Soggy cornflakes are bad enough, but imagine soggy flaked corns!

AND NOW DO MY LEFT FOOT, WIFE

One traditional shampoo treatment includes egg yolk. This is supposed to leave hair shiny, but sulphur in the egg can cause bleached blond hair to turn green!

Ear-cleaning routine

Take care when cleaning the ears. The delicate eardrum, just 2-3cm into the earhole, passes sounds to the hearing system and it's easily damaged.

HORRIBLE HEALTH WARNING!

The earhole is designed to produce wax to trap dirt and invading insects. One minor body design fault is that this wax can block the ear, and it's best to ask a doctor to squirt the wax out with water.

I MAKE THE MONSTER'S EARWAX INTO HORRIBLY TASTEFUL YELLOW-BROWN WAX CRAYONS, HA HA!

Nose-cleaning procedure

Oh dear, the Monster's lost his handkerchief…

GRRR!

PICK!

Sorry about that! The correct way to clean snot from the nose is to blow one nostril at a time gently into a handkerchief whilst pinching the other shut.

blow left

blow right

wipe!

Nail care for bodies

You'll need to cut your finger- and toenails. (Younger body owners need the help of an older owner.) The correct way to cut nails is straight across so there's no danger of the nail cutting into the skin as it gets longer.

This is a vital but rather unpleasant job — and you really wouldn't want to know what the Monster gets under his fingernails. Watch out for low-flying nail-clippings!

Refuelling your body

Body refuelling needs to be done morning, midday and evening. Without pit stops the body loses power and the brain runs data images of hamburgers and pizzas. The most vital stop is the morning one. The brain runs on a sugar called glucose. After a long night, glucose levels are low, so the brain feels groggy.

HERE'S SOME NICE HOT BLOOD GLUCOSE!

YUMMMEEE!

The brain contains a fuel-level sensor for glucose levels in the blood, known as appetite. When the body is low on glucose, it's called hunger, or 'feed me, I'm starving!'

Tooth-cleaning techniques

Use a small-headed soft nylon toothbrush to clean your teeth. Add a blob of toothpaste. Make small circular movements with the brush. Go right to the gums but avoid brushing them or they may bleed. Brush the biting surfaces and the sides of the teeth. Now rinse and spit.

IN THE BASIN, YOU BAD MONSTER!

SPIT!

ROTTEN
REFLEX ROADTEST

So you think you're razor sharp and ultra alert? Use this whizzy test to compare your reaction times with those of your friends and family. Are wrinklies really slower than spotty teenagers? Challenge on...

You will need:
- a 30cm ruler
- a notepad or paper
- a pen or pencil

1 Take the ruler and hold it between finger and thumb at the 30cm end, so it hangs downwards.

2 Ask someone to sit with one hand ready to pinch the ruler as you let go. Make sure they have their fingers poised at the 0cm mark. Tell them you're going to drop the ruler any time in the next 5 seconds. They must try to grab it between finger and thumb as quickly as possible before it falls to the ground.

3 Let go of the ruler whenever you choose within the 5 seconds.

4 When the ruler has been grabbed (assuming they didn't miss altogether and let it drop to the floor), record where the fingers are on the measure. About 5cm would be a very speedy reaction; 20cm plus is pretty rubbish!

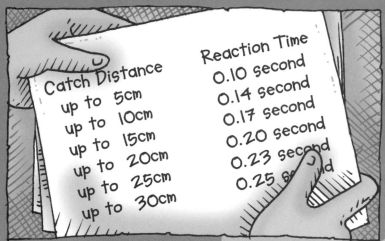

5 Draw a tick-box chart for name, age and so on to record all your results. Repeat the test on as many different people as you can. Let each person have five goes and record the best (shortest) catch for each.

6 Convert the recorded measurements to approximate reaction times, using this table. Which group of people have the quickest reaction times – boys or girls, young or old?

Body Scent Detection Quiz

So how well do you know your own body? Are you a budding body expert or a baffled body beginner?

1. Some body advice experts (known as doctors) detect diseases by sniffing the skin. What does gangrene (when infected body bits start to rot) smell like?

a) school dinner b) very old fish c) mouldy apples

2. In the USA, fir trees are sprayed with a substance to put off thieves. What does this stinking substance smell like?

a) skunk juice   b) fox wee   c) bad breath

3. In 2001, US military planners were working on extra-powerful stink bombs to control riots. In tests, what smell proved the most effective?

a) poo

b) sweaty feet smeared with rotting butter

c) vomit

4. A sensory analyst is trained to spot dozens of different smells. In one US company women analysts were given a disgusting duty. Did they have to...?

a) sniff the difference between old socks and maggoty cheese

b) sniff men's dirty, sweaty armpits

c) sit by a smelly pond and sniff out foul-smelling frogs

WELL I THINK YOU SMELL LOVELY!

THANKS!

Turn to page 60 to see the answers.

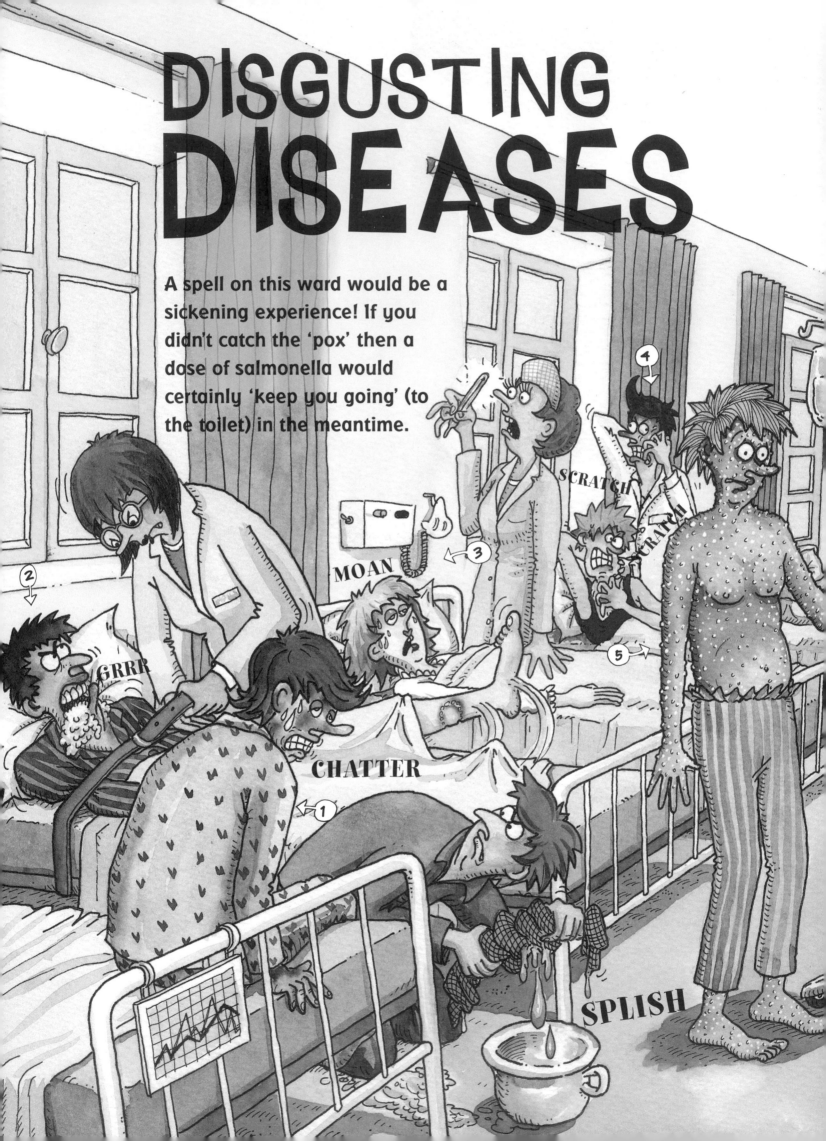

DIS-EASE HELL

1. This patient caught dengue fever in Africa. It's transmitted by mosquitoes. He has a raging fever and has just been sick on the floor.

2. Don't approach this madman – he's got rabies and is raving! The bite on his leg is a clue – and he's angry with the nurse for suggesting a bath... rabies victims are afraid of water.

3. This lady swam in water with rat's pee in it... and swallowed some! Now she's got Weil's (say Viles) disease. Without anitbiotics, it can be fatal.

4. This patient has generously shared his scabies with the doctor. These 'itch mites' jump between people and burrow into their skin to lay eggs.

5. This guy's got smallpox... but how? Vaccination has rid the world of this deadly disease – the last case was in 1977. It exists only in labs...

6. This patient's not hungry because he has Chagas disease, spread by a bug bite in South America. Treated early, he should survive!

7. Food poisoning from salmonella bacteria in a meal containing under-cooked fish is grinding this chap's guts. Don't block his way to the loo!

8. This grinning goon has lock-jaw after forgetting to get his tetanus jab after cutting himself deeply on something grubby.

9. The killer MRSA bacterium is on the bed. It's a super-bug as it's resistant to most antibiotics!

THE FRIGHTFUL FLU

Often confused with the common cold, flu is a much more unpleasant illness which, if you're really unlucky, can even be fatal…

FLU INFECTS MORE THAN 100 MILLION PEOPLE ALL OVER THE WORLD EVERY SINGLE YEAR.

COUGH!

SNEEZE!

SPLUTTER!

CROAK!

PASS THE TISSUES

SNIFFLE!

MOAN!

THE SINISTER SYMPTOMS OF THIS VILE VIRUS INCLUDE SORE THROAT, SWEATING, ACHES, PAINS, FEVER, CHILLS AND FATIGUE.

FLU IS INCREDIBLY INFECTIOUS AND IS SPREAD THROUGH THE AIR BY DISEASE-RIDDEN DROPLETS SNEEZED OR COUGHED OUT BY PEOPLE WHO ALREADY HAVE IT.

AAAA-TISH-OOOOO!

THANKS

THE VIRUS IS ESPECIALLY INFECTIOUS DURING COLD WEATHER AS IT CAN STAY ALIVE FOR LONGER AT LOW TEMPERATURES.

FLU'S BEEN RESPONSIBLE FOR SPREADING SICKNESS THROUGHOUT HISTORY. THE FAMOUS GREEK PHYSICIAN, HIPPOCRATES (HIP-OH-CRA-TEES), DESCRIBED ITS SYMPTOMS MORE THAN 2000 YEARS AGO.

ALTHOUGH IT'S NOT NICE, THE INFECTION IS NORMALLY OVER WITHIN A COUPLE OF WEEKS. BUT FOR SOME PEOPLE, SUCH AS YOUNG CHILDREN AND OLD PEOPLE, IT CAN BE VERY SERIOUS - EVEN DEADLY.

IT WAS THE COUGH THAT KNOCKED HIM OFF

SPLUTTER!

R.I.P TO DEAR OLD DOUG VICTIM OF A NASTY BUG

HE MUST BE SICK OF HIS JOB!.

SNIFFLE!

AAA-TISH-OO!

SHIVER!

WORLDWIDE, THE AVERAGE ANNUAL DEATH TOLL FROM FLU-RELATED ILLNESSES IS AROUND 500,000.

SOME BOFFINS THINK THAT THE BEASTLY BUG WAS BEHIND THE DISASTROUS DEFEAT OF SOLDIERS PROTECTING THE ANCIENT GREEK CITY OF ATHENS IN 404 BC.

THE NAME FLU COMES FROM THE WORD INFLUENZA* WHICH WAS FIRST USED BY 15TH CENTURY ITALIANS WHO THOUGHT THAT IT WAS CAUSED BY THE INFLUENCE OF THE STARS AND PLANETS...

IT'S ALL IN THE STARS. SNIFF!

RUBBISH! IF YOU'D KEPT THE WINDOW CLOSED WE'D NEVER HAVE CAUGHT THIS CURSED COLD.

BURP!

YOU'RE A BAD INFLUENCE!

...THEY LATER DECIDED IT HAD MORE TO DO WITH COLD WEATHER.

*INFLUENZA (IN-FLEW-EN-ZA) MEANS INFLUENCE IN ITALIAN.

EARLY REMEDIES FOR INFLUENZA INCLUDED DRINKING LIME JUICE, MAKING THE VICTIMS VOMIT AND GIVING THEM MEDICINE TO MAKE THEM POO.

BLEAUGH!

I'VE GOT THE RUNS!

LIME NOT ENJOYING THIS.

NEEDLESS TO SAY, NONE OF THEM WORKED.

FLU FIRST SPREAD RIGHT ACROSS THE GLOBE IN 1580. MANY PEOPLE DIED AND A COUPLE OF SPANISH CITIES WERE COMPLETELY WIPED-OUT.

THIS BLEEDIN' HURTS!

A POPULAR CURE AT THIS TIME INVOLVED TAKING BLOOD FROM THE BODIES OF FEVERISH PATIENTS. IT WASN'T VERY SUCCESSFUL.

THE WORST PANDEMIC* SO FAR STARTED IN 1918. IT LASTED FOR TWO YEARS AND KILLED UP TO 100 MILLION PEOPLE WORLDWIDE. IT EVEN SPREAD TO THE ARCTIC.

I BLAME THE SPANISH.

SPEAK UP, I CAN'T 'EAR YOU!

SPLUTTER COUGH

SOME SEVERE SIDE-EFFECTS OF THE SO-CALLED SPANISH FLU INCLUDED BLEEDING FROM THE NOSE, EARS, SKIN AND INSIDE THE STOMACH.

*A PANDEMIC (PAN-DEM-ICK) IS WHEN AN ILLNESS SPREADS ACROSS A LARGE AREA.

THE FIRST FLU VACCINE WAS PRODUCED IN THE 1940S. IT WAS MADE BY INJECTING A DEAD FLU VIRUS INTO A HEN'S EGG AND LEAVING IT TO GROW FOR A FEW DAYS.

IT'S AN EGGS-TRAORDINARY DEVELOPMENT!

CERTAINLY NOT TO BE SNIFFED AT!

FLU VIRUS

TENS OF MILLIONS OF EGGS ARE USED TO CREATE THE FLU VACCINE EVERY YEAR.

THERE'VE BEEN TWO MORE PANDEMICS SINCE 1918 - BOTH KILLED MILLIONS OF PEOPLE.

PSST! I'VE GOT FLU - PASS IT ON.

COUGH, SPLUTTER

DAILY BLO 19
ASIAN OUTB

DAILY BLO 1968
HONG KONG KILLER BUG SPREADING

THE FIENDISH FLU VIRUS CHANGES EVERY YEAR. SCIENTISTS AREN'T ALWAYS ABLE TO MAKE A VACCINE FAST ENOUGH TO STOP IT SPREADING.

TODAY, THE BIGGEST FLU THREAT IS FROM A VIRUS FIRST FOUND IN CHICKENS.

WHERE'S HEN-RY?

HE FLU AWAY...

BIRD FLU CAN SPREAD FROM BIRD TO HUMAN. IT HASN'T SPREAD FROM PERSON TO PERSON YET BUT THE BOFFINS ARE BOTHERED THAT ONE DAY IT WILL...

55

MAKE YOUR OWN BARFING BELLY

BEWARE OF MESSY EXPERIMENT

You will need:
- a balloon (the larger the balloon, the fatter your stomach!)
- a funnel
- a ripe banana
- a pencil
- a teaspoon
- a measuring jug
- vinegar
- bicarbonate of soda
- safety goggles

Most deadly diseases will make your tummy feel terrible – you may want to re-examine your dinner...

PFFFSSS

ROLL

1 Blow up the balloon and let the air out a few times to make the balloon saggy and baggy.

SAG!

new balloon

2 Now roll the neck of the balloon over the bottom of the funnel. Peel a ripe banana.

SQUISH

SQUELCH

3 Break the banana up into small pieces and pop them into the funnel. If your balloon-stomach has problems 'eating' the banana, help it along by squishing the banana chunks down with the pencil.

4 Follow the yummy banana meal down with two teaspoons of bicarbonate of soda. Then squish and squash the stomach a few times with your hand. This mashes and churns the banana like your teeth and stomach do in real life.

SWELL

BLEURGH!

6 You can let the gas out to make your stomach burp. And when you squeeze it, your sickly stomach will blow chunks of half-digested banana everywhere!

5 Put on your safety goggles. Measure out 50ml of vinegar into your jug and pour it down the funnel. Give the neck of the balloon a quick twist once the vinegar's gone in to stop anything coming back out. Take out the funnel and then give the balloon a brisk shake.

Go to the Puzzle answers on page 60 to discover the science behind this sick experiment.

HORRIBLE HEALTH WARNING!

Wear safety googles and make sure you do this experiment outdoors. Hold the barfing belly well away from your face and eyes. It may put you off bananas forever!

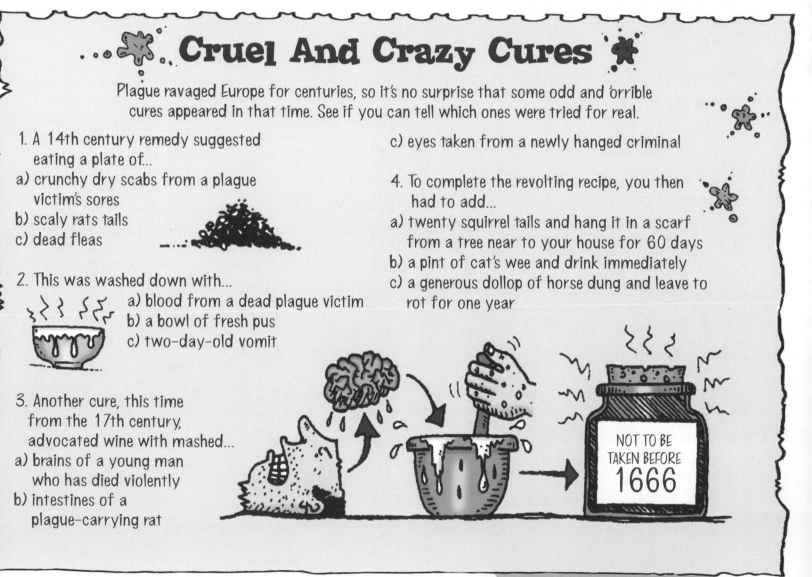

...✲.·. Cruel And Crazy Cures ✲

Plague ravaged Europe for centuries, so it's no surprise that some odd and 'orrible cures appeared in that time. See if you can tell which ones were tried for real.

1. A 14th century remedy suggested eating a plate of...
a) crunchy dry scabs from a plague victim's sores
b) scaly rats tails
c) dead fleas

2. This was washed down with...
a) blood from a dead plague victim
b) a bowl of fresh pus
c) two-day-old vomit

3. Another cure, this time from the 17th century, advocated wine with mashed...
a) brains of a young man who has died violently
b) intestines of a plague-carrying rat

c) eyes taken from a newly hanged criminal

4. To complete the revolting recipe, you then had to add...
a) twenty squirrel tails and hang it in a scarf from a tree near to your house for 60 days
b) a pint of cat's wee and drink immediately
c) a generous dollop of horse dung and leave to rot for one year

NOT TO BE TAKEN BEFORE 1666

Turn to page 60 to see the answers.

QUARANTINE WARD

Before you enter this area, you might want to heed a warning. Some disease stories are so deadly and disgusting they have to be separated from the rest of the annual!

Don't Feel Like Chicken Tonight!

In 1997 something terrifying happened. Scientists in Hong Kong found a new type of flu that attacked chickens. The virus that caused the flu was similar to the one that killed thousands of people in 1918. In just a few months, say the experts, the virus could have changed its DNA so that it could attack people. It could have swept around the world carried inside passengers on jet planes. And it might have killed hundreds of millions of people.

As things turned out, luckily it didn't. The scientists killed all the chickens that carried the disease and stopped it spreading – this time!

NEWS
ALL HONG KONG CHICKENS KILLED!

EGGS $100,000 EACH

Plague Bravery

In the English village of Eyam in 1665 a bundle of cloth sent from the plague-stricken city of London brought fleas and the plague. Within four days the man who had received the cloth was dead.

Bravely, the villagers decided to quarantine their village, letting no one in or out so that the plague wouldn't spread. Then one by one, they died. By the following spring, of the 350 villagers, just 84 were left alive. But it was thanks to their bravery that the plague spread no further in their area.

Slow but Sneaky

Diseases are usually unpleasant, often deadly, but rarely spread quickly. Why? There are exceptions – like the plague or 1918 flu epidemic – but generally diseases don't spread rapidly, for a horribly good reason. If people died in five minutes then the germs would be buried with their first victim and never spread. And being buried alive is nasty – even for a germ.

ARGH! GROAN! **RIP** SID SNUFFIT WHO DIED IN FIVE MINUTES FLAT. MOAN! GASP! ERK!

But if the disease spreads gradually over a period of months or years, then there is more time for other people to come into contact with it and catch it! Sneaky!

Crazy Plagueing

During the plague of the Middle Ages, people had some nutty ideas about preventing the spread of the disease. Here's the latest anti-plague fashion of 1348, and guess what – it didn't even work!

beak full of nice smelling herbs

mask

wand for checking a victim's pulse

long leather gloves

leather gown

SCIENTIFIC NOTE
This gear didn't stop the fleas biting the doctor and causing plague.

Feeling Pee-ved

In 1348 people thought the plague was caused by a nasty smell in the air. This smell could be kept out by smoke (they beat children at Eton School, England for not smoking!) ringing bells, letting birds fly around the room, and releasing bottled farts (which would also get rid of your friends!)

DING! DONG!

At the time, bathing in water was seen as a bad idea (some stinky readers may agree), but instead doctors thought they could keep the plague away by bathing in vinegar, your own pee (and by drinking anything left over) or even in goats' pee! Imagine how pee-ved you'd feel if it didn't work!

Cringey Cholera

WARNING!
The following stories will make you cringe!
Not to be read at mealtimes!

1. Even though it was proved otherwise, some scientists refused to believe that cholera was caused by a germ. German scientist Max von Pettenkofer (1818-1901) thought that the disease was caused by chemicals. To prove his theory he actually drank a revolting mixture of germs taken from the diarrhoea of a cholera victim! Unsurprisingly Max got mild diarrhoea which he claimed was nothing to do with the cholera. Yeah, right.

NOT BAD, PERHAPS A LITTLE MORE PEPPER

2. This experience was not unique. A nurse told Dr John Snow how one night she was tired after a long day nursing cholera patients and she felt like a drink. She picked up a large cup of tea and gulped it down. Only then did she realise that it wasn't tea she was drinking... it was a potty full of diarrhoea! The nurse survived, but she went a bit potty!

CUP OF TEA, DOCTOR?

But why didn't Max and the nurse get cholera? Well, they were being protected by their stomachs. Yes, the human stomach makes a strong acid that dissolves most of the cholera germs. What a solution!

PUZZLE ANSWERS

Brilliant boffin or braindead buffoon? Rate yourself by checking the answers plus uncover the science secrets behind the sick tricks in this appalling annual.

BECOME A MIND READER p15

Here's how the mind-reading works:

First you got your volunteer to multiply by 9 a number between 1 and 10. If you get a two-digit number, they always add to make 9. So, when you subtract 5, you should always get 4. If you got a single-digit number, which could be 9 itself (9x1), then you just subtracted 5 from it to get 4.

The fourth letter of the alphabet, 'd', gets most people to think of Denmark, unless of course they're a geography teacher.

Most people will think of an 'elephant' first, when asked to think of an animal beginning with 'e'. Don't let them change their mind if you get the required reply. And, while they're thinking of an elephant's colour you can say, "Hey, there are no grey elephants in Denmark."

SPOT THE DIFFERENCE p17

TASTY OR SMELLY? p28

While your tastebuds identify the four basic tastes of sour, sweet, bitter and salty, it's the smell receptors in the top of your nose that really help you recognise subtle flavours. Seventy-five percent of your sense of taste comes from your sense of smell.

RECKLESS REFLEXES p29

Reflexes - 1, 2, 4, 6
Non-reflexes - 3, 5, 8, 7

TWITCHY WORDSEARCH p29

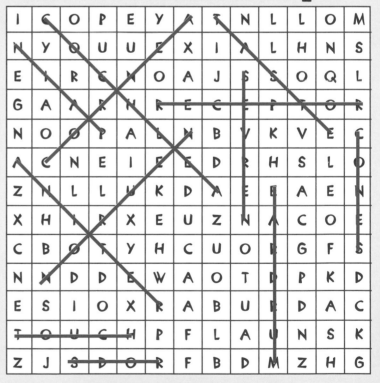

The hidden phrase is: THE CAT'S WHISKERS

FEELING FOUL p39

The power of suggestion should make them guess: eyeballs (tomatoes), skin (clingfilm), brains (eggs), fingers (sausages), teeth (popcorn).

SPOT THE DIFFERENCE p39

WICKED WORDSEARCH p39

G	J	H	T	L	M	N	D	X		P	M	K	
T	A	S	C	U	I	A	N	D	N	G	U	D	
Y	E	L	T	A	N	Y	E	E	T	O	N	P	
T	I	C	I	C	M	N	E	B	E	I	U	V	
V	E	Q	R	B	U	Q	Z	R	S	O	J	Y	
R	I	E	D	M	I	W	T	F	M	E	P	
V	A	X	Z	V	R	A	I	S	C	J	A	
S	M	O	U	T	H	E	R	M	N	N	J	
M	U	E	I	Y	A	C	R	E	A	E	Y	
L	L	A	I	O	M	V	M	T	E	P	J	M	
H	G	N	T	U	C	O	I	U	M	R	W	E	
D	B	I	L	E	F	U	T	L	M	T	O	J	
M	U	N	E	D	O	U	D	S	L	I	A	R	

BODY SCENT QUIZ p51

1 c) Gangrene smells like mouldy apples. The disease typhoid smells like baking bread and yellow fever smells like fresh meat.

2 b) The thieves were cutting down the trees and selling them as Christmas trees. People didn't want trees that smelled of wee, so the thieves were foxed.

3 a) According to scientist Pam Dalton, who led the stink-bomb project, an ultra-powerful pooey pong made volunteers scream and curse, especially when mixed with rotting onions.

4 b) The women had to sniff the sweaty armpits of male bodies to test if a deodorant was working. I bet that job got up their noses!

CRUEL AND CRAZY CURES p57

1.a   2.b   3.a   4.c

BARFING BELLY p56

Here's the science behind this experiement: A real stomach holds up to 1.5 litres of food in a chewed-up, spit-slobbered mix. When you mashed the banana, you were doing the job of the teeth and stomach. Like the vinegar you added, the stomach makes an acid that dissolves food. Muscles hold the top and bottom openings closed and stop you sicking up food as your stomach squelches. The balloon didn't have a muscle, so you twisted its neck. Air can escape from the stomach as a burp. The bicarbonate of soda and vinegar made gas and the stomach swelled. When you're sick, muscles around the stomach squeeze like your hand squeezing the balloon. They squeeze so hard that the squirting sick splatters out. Bleeuurrrgh!